Copyright © 2023 by Jasmine Bishop

All rights reserved. No part of this publication may be reproduced, distributed, or transmitted in any form or by any means, including photocopying, recording, or other electronic or mechanical methods without the prior written permission of the publisher except in the case of brief quotations embodied in critical reviews and certain other noncommercial uses permitted by copyright law.

Adherence to all applicable laws and regulations including international business practices, advertising, and all other aspects of doing business in the US, Canada, or any other jurisdiction is the sole responsibility of the purchaser or reader.

Though this product was created by a licensed mental health therapist, it is not a substitute for a relationship with a licensed mental health professional. This is a tool meant to be paired with personal self-help efforts or to leverage progress made in an outside therapeutic relationship with a professional. The author bears no responsibility for the misuse of the product outside of the above directions.

More journals from this author:
Know Your Feelings Journal
Daily Reflection Challenge Journal
Feeling Myself Journal
Feelings are not Facts

olivetreehealthllc.com

Paperback ISBN: 979-8-9882406-1-7

Feelings Chart

Because feelings aren't easy
(feel free to add your own colors for each feeling)

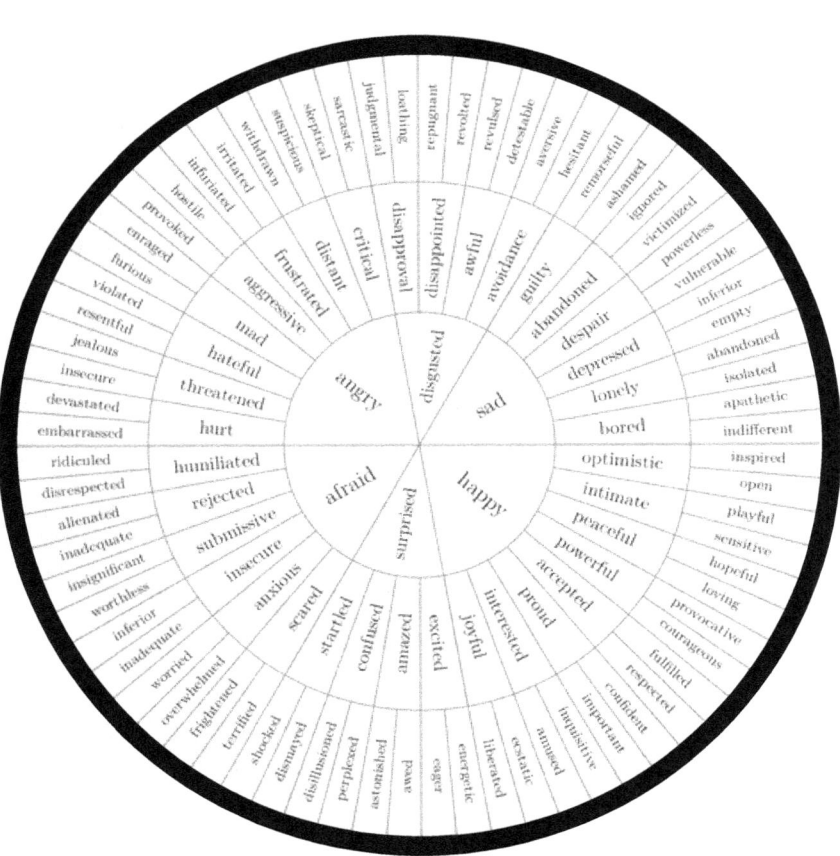

Tips for finding a therapist who is a good fit:

Think about your budget for therapy

If it impacts you, check with your insurance to see if they cover mental health services

Google therapists in your area who work with what you want to address in therapy

Identify traits in a person that will prevent you from talking freely

Identify traits that help you feel comfortable

Schedule a consultation with your potential therapist

Choose the person who you can see yourself opening up to (trust your gut)

This journal is not meant to replace therapy with a licensed mental health professional but to be paired with therapy to maximize accountability and progress.

Goals for Therapy

What do you want from therapy and how will you know once you've achieved that goal?

Be specific about how you will be thinking, feeling, behaving. What will your life look like?

_____
_____
_____
_____
_____
_____
_____
_____
_____
_____
_____
_____
_____
_____
_____
_____
_____
_____
_____
_____
_____
_____
_____
_____

Review Us!

Olive Tree Health is a Black woman-owned small business.

We'd *love* it if you supported us by telling us what you think about our journal!

Use this QR code to leave us a review and you'll get a free wellness tool!

Wellness Plan

Support people/ items in my life:

_____
_____

Triggers:

_____
_____

Activities I do that help me be peaceful and grounded:

_____
_____

How do I want to be cared for during a crisis?

_____
_____

What makes me feel safe to navigate conflict or hard conversations in relationships (therapy included)?

_____
_____

Hotlines or warmlines I can call if I have an emergency:

SAMHSA : 1-800-487-4889
Crisis Hotline : 988
Nat. Mental Health Hotline: 866-903-3787
Mental Health America Textline: Text "MHA" to 741-741

Contact info for mental health resources in my area:

_____
_____
_____

First Session

Major life events (trauma, loss, family changes, important relationships, etc.)

_____
_____
_____
_____
_____
_____
_____
_____

What should the therapist know about your learning style and personality?

_____
_____
_____

How would you prefer the therapist engage you when you are triggered?

_____
_____
_____

Questions for the therapist:

_____
_____
_____

Date: _____

Situations, struggles, and wins to bring up in session:

Homework and realizations to sit with before next session:

Date: _____

Situations, struggles, and wins to bring up in session:

_____
_____
_____
_____
_____
_____
_____
_____
_____
_____
_____
_____
_____

Homework and realizations to sit with before next session:

_____
_____
_____
_____
_____
_____
_____
_____
_____
_____
_____
_____
_____

Date: _____

Situations, struggles, and wins to bring up in session:

Homework and realizations to sit with before next session:

Date: _____

Situations, struggles, and wins to bring up in session:

_____
_____
_____
_____
_____
_____
_____
_____
_____
_____
_____
_____

Homework and realizations to sit with before next session:

_____
_____
_____
_____
_____
_____
_____
_____
_____
_____
_____

Date: _____

Situations, struggles, and wins to bring up in session:

_____
_____
_____
_____
_____
_____
_____
_____
_____
_____
_____
_____
_____
_____

Homework and realizations to sit with before next session:

_____
_____
_____
_____
_____
_____
_____
_____
_____
_____
_____
_____
_____
_____

Date: _____

Situations, struggles, and wins to bring up in session:

_____
_____
_____
_____
_____
_____
_____
_____
_____
_____
_____
_____
_____

Homework and realizations to sit with before next session:

_____
_____
_____
_____
_____
_____
_____
_____
_____
_____
_____
_____

Date: _____

Situations, struggles, and wins to bring up in session:

_____
_____
_____
_____
_____
_____
_____
_____
_____
_____
_____
_____

Homework and realizations to sit with before next session:

_____
_____
_____
_____
_____
_____
_____
_____
_____
_____
_____
_____

Date: _____

Situations, struggles, and wins to bring up in session:

_____
_____
_____
_____
_____
_____
_____
_____
_____
_____
_____
_____

Homework and realizations to sit with before next session:

_____
_____
_____
_____
_____
_____
_____
_____
_____
_____
_____
_____

Date: _____

Situations, struggles, and wins to bring up in session:

_____
_____
_____
_____
_____
_____
_____
_____
_____
_____
_____
_____

Homework and realizations to sit with before next session:

_____
_____
_____
_____
_____
_____
_____
_____
_____
_____
_____
_____

Date: _____

Situations, struggles, and wins to bring up in session:

_____
_____
_____
_____
_____
_____
_____
_____
_____
_____
_____

Homework and realizations to sit with before next session:

_____
_____
_____
_____
_____
_____
_____
_____
_____
_____
_____

Date: _____

Situations, struggles, and wins to bring up in session:

_____
_____
_____
_____
_____
_____
_____
_____
_____
_____
_____
_____

Homework and realizations to sit with before next session:

_____
_____
_____
_____
_____
_____
_____
_____
_____
_____
_____
_____

Date: _____

Situations, struggles, and wins to bring up in session:

_____
_____
_____
_____
_____
_____
_____
_____
_____
_____
_____
_____

Homework and realizations to sit with before next session:

_____
_____
_____
_____
_____
_____
_____
_____
_____
_____
_____
_____
_____
_____

Date: _____

Situations, struggles, and wins to bring up in session:

_____
_____
_____
_____
_____
_____
_____
_____
_____
_____
_____
_____
_____
_____

Homework and realizations to sit with before next session:

_____
_____
_____
_____
_____
_____
_____
_____
_____
_____
_____
_____
_____
_____

Date: _____

Situations, struggles, and wins to bring up in session:

_____
_____
_____
_____
_____
_____
_____
_____
_____
_____
_____
_____

Homework and realizations to sit with before next session:

_____
_____
_____
_____
_____
_____
_____
_____
_____
_____
_____
_____

Date: _____

Situations, struggles, and wins to bring up in session:

_____
_____
_____
_____
_____
_____
_____
_____
_____
_____
_____

Homework and realizations to sit with before next session:

_____
_____
_____
_____
_____
_____
_____
_____
_____
_____
_____

Date: _____

Situations, struggles, and wins to bring up in session:

Homework and realizations to sit with before next session:

Date: _____

Situations, struggles, and wins to bring up in session:

_____
_____
_____
_____
_____
_____
_____
_____
_____
_____
_____

Homework and realizations to sit with before next session:

_____
_____
_____
_____
_____
_____
_____
_____
_____
_____
_____
_____

Date: _____

Situations, struggles, and wins to bring up in session:

_____
_____
_____
_____
_____
_____
_____
_____
_____
_____
_____
_____
_____

Homework and realizations to sit with before next session:

_____
_____
_____
_____
_____
_____
_____
_____
_____
_____
_____
_____
_____

Date: _____

Situations, struggles, and wins to bring up in session:

Homework and realizations to sit with before next session:

Date: _____

Situations, struggles, and wins to bring up in session:

_____
_____
_____
_____
_____
_____
_____
_____
_____
_____
_____
_____
_____
_____

Homework and realizations to sit with before next session:

_____
_____
_____
_____
_____
_____
_____
_____
_____
_____
_____
_____
_____

Date: _____

Situations, struggles, and wins to bring up in session:

_____
_____
_____
_____
_____
_____
_____
_____
_____
_____
_____

Homework and realizations to sit with before next session:

_____
_____
_____
_____
_____
_____
_____
_____
_____
_____
_____
_____

Date: _____

Situations, struggles, and wins to bring up in session:

_____
_____
_____
_____
_____
_____
_____
_____
_____
_____
_____
_____

Homework and realizations to sit with before next session:

_____
_____
_____
_____
_____
_____
_____
_____
_____
_____
_____
_____

Date: _____

Situations, struggles, and wins to bring up in session:

Homework and realizations to sit with before next session:

Date: _____

Situations, struggles, and wins to bring up in session:

_____
_____
_____
_____
_____
_____
_____
_____
_____
_____
_____
_____

Homework and realizations to sit with before next session:

_____
_____
_____
_____
_____
_____
_____
_____
_____
_____
_____
_____

Date: _____

Situations, struggles, and wins to bring up in session:

_____
_____
_____
_____
_____
_____
_____
_____
_____
_____
_____

Homework and realizations to sit with before next session:

_____
_____
_____
_____
_____
_____
_____
_____
_____

Date: _____

Situations, struggles, and wins to bring up in session:

_____
_____
_____
_____
_____
_____
_____
_____
_____
_____
_____
_____
_____
_____

Homework and realizations to sit with before next session:

_____
_____
_____
_____
_____
_____
_____
_____
_____
_____
_____
_____
_____
_____

Date: _____

Situations, struggles, and wins to bring up in session:

_____
_____
_____
_____
_____
_____
_____
_____
_____
_____
_____
_____

Homework and realizations to sit with before next session:

_____
_____
_____
_____
_____
_____
_____
_____
_____
_____
_____
_____

Date: _____

Situations, struggles, and wins to bring up in session:

_____
_____
_____
_____
_____
_____
_____
_____
_____
_____
_____

Homework and realizations to sit with before next session:

_____
_____
_____
_____
_____
_____
_____
_____
_____
_____
_____

Date: _____

Situations, struggles, and wins to bring up in session:

_____
_____
_____
_____
_____
_____
_____
_____
_____
_____
_____
_____

Homework and realizations to sit with before next session:

_____
_____
_____
_____
_____
_____
_____
_____
_____
_____
_____
_____
_____

Date: _____

Situations, struggles, and wins to bring up in session:

_____
_____
_____
_____
_____
_____
_____
_____
_____
_____
_____

Homework and realizations to sit with before next session:

_____
_____
_____
_____
_____
_____
_____
_____
_____
_____
_____

Date: _____

Situations, struggles, and wins to bring up in session:

_____
_____
_____
_____
_____
_____
_____
_____
_____
_____
_____
_____

Homework and realizations to sit with before next session:

_____
_____
_____
_____
_____
_____
_____
_____
_____
_____
_____
_____

Date: _____

Situations, struggles, and wins to bring up in session:

_____
_____
_____
_____
_____
_____
_____
_____
_____
_____
_____
_____

Homework and realizations to sit with before next session:

_____
_____
_____
_____
_____
_____
_____
_____
_____
_____
_____
_____

Date: _____

Situations, struggles, and wins to bring up in session:

_____
_____
_____
_____
_____
_____
_____
_____
_____
_____
_____
_____

Homework and realizations to sit with before next session:

_____
_____
_____
_____
_____
_____
_____
_____
_____
_____
_____
_____

Date: _____

Situations, struggles, and wins to bring up in session:

_____
_____
_____
_____
_____
_____
_____
_____
_____
_____
_____
_____
_____

Homework and realizations to sit with before next session:

_____
_____
_____
_____
_____
_____
_____
_____
_____
_____
_____
_____
_____

Date: _____

Situations, struggles, and wins to bring up in session:

_____
_____
_____
_____
_____
_____
_____
_____
_____
_____
_____
_____

Homework and realizations to sit with before next session:

_____
_____
_____
_____
_____
_____
_____
_____
_____
_____
_____
_____

Date: _____

Situations, struggles, and wins to bring up in session:

_____
_____
_____
_____
_____
_____
_____
_____
_____
_____

Homework and realizations to sit with before next session:

_____
_____
_____
_____
_____
_____
_____
_____
_____
_____

Date: _____

Situations, struggles, and wins to bring up in session:

_____
_____
_____
_____
_____
_____
_____
_____
_____
_____

Homework and realizations to sit with before next session:

_____
_____
_____
_____
_____
_____
_____
_____
_____
_____
_____

Date: _____

Situations, struggles, and wins to bring up in session:

_____
_____
_____
_____
_____
_____
_____
_____
_____
_____
_____
_____
_____
_____

Homework and realizations to sit with before next session:

_____
_____
_____
_____
_____
_____
_____
_____
_____
_____
_____
_____
_____
_____

Date: _____

Situations, struggles, and wins to bring up in session:

_____
_____
_____
_____
_____
_____
_____
_____
_____
_____
_____

Homework and realizations to sit with before next session:

_____
_____
_____
_____
_____
_____
_____
_____
_____
_____
_____

Date: _____

Situations, struggles, and wins to bring up in session:

_____
_____
_____
_____
_____
_____
_____
_____
_____
_____
_____
_____
_____

Homework and realizations to sit with before next session:

_____
_____
_____
_____
_____
_____
_____
_____
_____
_____
_____
_____

Date: _____

Situations, struggles, and wins to bring up in session:

_____
_____
_____
_____
_____
_____
_____
_____
_____
_____
_____
_____
_____
_____

Homework and realizations to sit with before next session:

_____
_____
_____
_____
_____
_____
_____
_____
_____
_____
_____
_____
_____

Date: _____

Situations, struggles, and wins to bring up in session:

_____
_____
_____
_____
_____
_____
_____
_____
_____
_____
_____
_____
_____

Homework and realizations to sit with before next session:

_____
_____
_____
_____
_____
_____
_____
_____
_____
_____
_____

Date: _____

Situations, struggles, and wins to bring up in session:

_____
_____
_____
_____
_____
_____
_____
_____
_____
_____
_____
_____

Homework and realizations to sit with before next session:

_____
_____
_____
_____
_____
_____
_____
_____
_____
_____
_____
_____
_____
_____

Date: _____

Situations, struggles, and wins to bring up in session:

_____
_____
_____
_____
_____
_____
_____
_____
_____
_____
_____
_____

Homework and realizations to sit with before next session:

_____
_____
_____
_____
_____
_____
_____
_____
_____
_____
_____
_____

Date: _____

Situations, struggles, and wins to bring up in session:

_____
_____
_____
_____
_____
_____
_____
_____
_____
_____
_____
_____
_____

Homework and realizations to sit with before next session:

_____
_____
_____
_____
_____
_____
_____
_____
_____
_____
_____
_____
_____
_____

Date: _____

Situations, struggles, and wins to bring up in session:

_____
_____
_____
_____
_____
_____
_____
_____
_____
_____
_____
_____

Homework and realizations to sit with before next session:

_____
_____
_____
_____
_____
_____
_____
_____
_____
_____
_____
_____

Date: _____

Situations, struggles, and wins to bring up in session:

_____
_____
_____
_____
_____
_____
_____
_____
_____
_____
_____
_____

Homework and realizations to sit with before next session:

_____
_____
_____
_____
_____
_____
_____
_____
_____
_____
_____
_____

Date: _____

Situations, struggles, and wins to bring up in session:

_____
_____
_____
_____
_____
_____
_____
_____
_____
_____
_____

Homework and realizations to sit with before next session:

_____
_____
_____
_____
_____
_____
_____
_____
_____
_____
_____
_____

Date: _____

Situations, struggles, and wins to bring up in session:

_____
_____
_____
_____
_____
_____
_____
_____
_____
_____
_____

Homework and realizations to sit with before next session:

_____
_____
_____
_____
_____
_____
_____
_____
_____
_____
_____

Date: _____

Situations, struggles, and wins to bring up in session:

_____
_____
_____
_____
_____
_____
_____
_____
_____
_____
_____

Homework and realizations to sit with before next session:

_____
_____
_____
_____
_____
_____
_____
_____
_____
_____
_____

Date: _____

Situations, struggles, and wins to bring up in session:

___

Homework and realizations to sit with before next session:

___

Date: _____

Situations, struggles, and wins to bring up in session:

_____
_____
_____
_____
_____
_____
_____
_____
_____
_____
_____
_____
_____

Homework and realizations to sit with before next session:

_____
_____
_____
_____
_____
_____
_____
_____
_____
_____
_____
_____
_____

Date: _____

Situations, struggles, and wins to bring up in session:

_____
_____
_____
_____
_____
_____
_____
_____
_____
_____
_____

Homework and realizations to sit with before next session:

_____
_____
_____
_____
_____
_____
_____
_____
_____
_____
_____

Date: _____

Situations, struggles, and wins to bring up in session:

_____
_____
_____
_____
_____
_____
_____
_____
_____
_____
_____
_____

Homework and realizations to sit with before next session:

_____
_____
_____
_____
_____
_____
_____
_____
_____
_____
_____
_____

Date: _____

Situations, struggles, and wins to bring up in session:

_____
_____
_____
_____
_____
_____
_____
_____
_____
_____
_____
_____
_____

Homework and realizations to sit with before next session:

_____
_____
_____
_____
_____
_____
_____
_____
_____
_____
_____
_____
_____

Date: _____

Situations, struggles, and wins to bring up in session:

_____
_____
_____
_____
_____
_____
_____
_____
_____
_____
_____
_____
_____

Homework and realizations to sit with before next session:

_____
_____
_____
_____
_____
_____
_____
_____
_____
_____
_____
_____
_____

Date: _____

Situations, struggles, and wins to bring up in session:

_____
_____
_____
_____
_____
_____
_____
_____
_____
_____

Homework and realizations to sit with before next session:

_____
_____
_____
_____
_____
_____
_____
_____
_____
_____

Date: _____

Situations, struggles, and wins to bring up in session:

_____
_____
_____
_____
_____
_____
_____
_____
_____
_____
_____

Homework and realizations to sit with before next session:

_____
_____
_____
_____
_____
_____
_____
_____
_____
_____
_____
_____

Date: _____

Situations, struggles, and wins to bring up in session:

Homework and realizations to sit with before next session:

Date: _____

Situations, struggles, and wins to bring up in session:

_____
_____
_____
_____
_____
_____
_____
_____
_____
_____
_____
_____
_____

Homework and realizations to sit with before next session:

_____
_____
_____
_____
_____
_____
_____
_____
_____
_____
_____
_____
_____

Date: _____

Situations, struggles, and wins to bring up in session:

_____
_____
_____
_____
_____
_____
_____
_____
_____
_____
_____
_____

Homework and realizations to sit with before next session:

_____
_____
_____
_____
_____
_____
_____
_____
_____
_____
_____
_____

Date: _____

Situations, struggles, and wins to bring up in session:

_____
_____
_____
_____
_____
_____
_____
_____
_____
_____
_____
_____

Homework and realizations to sit with before next session:

_____
_____
_____
_____
_____
_____
_____
_____
_____
_____
_____
_____

Date: _____

Situations, struggles, and wins to bring up in session:

_____
_____
_____
_____
_____
_____
_____
_____
_____
_____
_____

Homework and realizations to sit with before next session:

_____
_____
_____
_____
_____
_____
_____
_____
_____
_____
_____
_____

Date: _____

Situations, struggles, and wins to bring up in session:

_____
_____
_____
_____
_____
_____
_____
_____
_____
_____
_____
_____
_____

Homework and realizations to sit with before next session:

_____
_____
_____
_____
_____
_____
_____
_____
_____
_____
_____
_____
_____

Date: _____

Situations, struggles, and wins to bring up in session:

_____
_____
_____
_____
_____
_____
_____
_____
_____
_____
_____
_____

Homework and realizations to sit with before next session:

_____
_____
_____
_____
_____
_____
_____
_____
_____
_____
_____

Date: _____

Situations, struggles, and wins to bring up in session:

_____
_____
_____
_____
_____
_____
_____
_____
_____
_____
_____
_____
_____
_____

Homework and realizations to sit with before next session:

_____
_____
_____
_____
_____
_____
_____
_____
_____
_____
_____
_____
_____
_____

Date: _____

Situations, struggles, and wins to bring up in session:

_____
_____
_____
_____
_____
_____
_____
_____
_____
_____
_____
_____

Homework and realizations to sit with before next session:

_____
_____
_____
_____
_____
_____
_____
_____
_____
_____
_____
_____

Date: _____

Situations, struggles, and wins to bring up in session:

_____
_____
_____
_____
_____
_____
_____
_____
_____
_____
_____
_____

Homework and realizations to sit with before next session:

_____
_____
_____
_____
_____
_____
_____
_____
_____
_____
_____
_____

Date: _____

Situations, struggles, and wins to bring up in session:

___

___

___

___

___

___

___

___

___

___

___

___

___

___

Homework and realizations to sit with before next session:

___

___

___

___

___

___

___

___

___

___

___

___

___

___

Date: _____

Situations, struggles, and wins to bring up in session:

_____
_____
_____
_____
_____
_____
_____
_____
_____
_____
_____
_____
_____
_____

Homework and realizations to sit with before next session:

_____
_____
_____
_____
_____
_____
_____
_____
_____
_____
_____
_____

Date: _____

Situations, struggles, and wins to bring up in session:

_____
_____
_____
_____
_____
_____
_____
_____
_____
_____
_____
_____
_____

Homework and realizations to sit with before next session:

_____
_____
_____
_____
_____
_____
_____
_____
_____
_____
_____
_____

Date: _____

Situations, struggles, and wins to bring up in session:

_____
_____
_____
_____
_____
_____
_____
_____
_____
_____

Homework and realizations to sit with before next session:

_____
_____
_____
_____
_____
_____
_____
_____
_____
_____

Date: _____

Situations, struggles, and wins to bring up in session:

_____
_____
_____
_____
_____
_____
_____
_____
_____
_____
_____
_____

Homework and realizations to sit with before next session:

_____
_____
_____
_____
_____
_____
_____
_____
_____
_____
_____
_____

Date: _____

Situations, struggles, and wins to bring up in session:

_____
_____
_____
_____
_____
_____
_____
_____
_____
_____
_____
_____

Homework and realizations to sit with before next session:

_____
_____
_____
_____
_____
_____
_____
_____
_____
_____
_____
_____

Date: _____

Situations, struggles, and wins to bring up in session:

_____
_____
_____
_____
_____
_____
_____
_____
_____
_____
_____
_____
_____

Homework and realizations to sit with before next session:

_____
_____
_____
_____
_____
_____
_____
_____
_____
_____
_____
_____

Date: _____

Situations, struggles, and wins to bring up in session:

_____
_____
_____
_____
_____
_____
_____
_____
_____
_____
_____

Homework and realizations to sit with before next session:

_____
_____
_____
_____
_____
_____
_____
_____
_____
_____
_____

Date: _____

Situations, struggles, and wins to bring up in session:

_____
_____
_____
_____
_____
_____
_____
_____
_____
_____
_____
_____

Homework and realizations to sit with before next session:

_____
_____
_____
_____
_____
_____
_____
_____
_____
_____
_____
_____
_____

Date: _____

Situations, struggles, and wins to bring up in session:

_____
_____
_____
_____
_____
_____
_____
_____
_____
_____
_____
_____

Homework and realizations to sit with before next session:

_____
_____
_____
_____
_____
_____
_____
_____
_____
_____
_____
_____

Date: _____

Situations, struggles, and wins to bring up in session:

_____
_____
_____
_____
_____
_____
_____
_____
_____
_____
_____
_____

Homework and realizations to sit with before next session:

_____
_____
_____
_____
_____
_____
_____
_____
_____
_____
_____
_____

Date: _____

Situations, struggles, and wins to bring up in session:

_____
_____
_____
_____
_____
_____
_____
_____
_____
_____
_____
_____
_____

Homework and realizations to sit with before next session:

_____
_____
_____
_____
_____
_____
_____
_____
_____
_____
_____
_____
_____

Date: _____

Situations, struggles, and wins to bring up in session:

_____
_____
_____
_____
_____
_____
_____
_____
_____
_____
_____

Homework and realizations to sit with before next session:

_____
_____
_____
_____
_____
_____
_____
_____
_____
_____
_____
_____

Date: _____

Situations, struggles, and wins to bring up in session:

_____
_____
_____
_____
_____
_____
_____
_____
_____
_____
_____
_____
_____

Homework and realizations to sit with before next session:

_____
_____
_____
_____
_____
_____
_____
_____
_____
_____
_____
_____
_____

Date: _____

Situations, struggles, and wins to bring up in session:

Homework and realizations to sit with before next session:

Date: _____

Situations, struggles, and wins to bring up in session:

_____
_____
_____
_____
_____
_____
_____
_____
_____
_____
_____
_____

Homework and realizations to sit with before next session:

_____
_____
_____
_____
_____
_____
_____
_____
_____
_____
_____
_____

Date: _____

Situations, struggles, and wins to bring up in session:

_____
_____
_____
_____
_____
_____
_____
_____
_____
_____
_____
_____

Homework and realizations to sit with before next session:

_____
_____
_____
_____
_____
_____
_____
_____
_____
_____
_____
_____

Date: _____

Situations, struggles, and wins to bring up in session:

_____
_____
_____
_____
_____
_____
_____
_____
_____
_____
_____
_____

Homework and realizations to sit with before next session:

_____
_____
_____
_____
_____
_____
_____
_____
_____
_____
_____

Date: _____

Situations, struggles, and wins to bring up in session:

_____
_____
_____
_____
_____
_____
_____
_____
_____
_____
_____

Homework and realizations to sit with before next session:

_____
_____
_____
_____
_____
_____
_____
_____
_____
_____
_____

Date: _____

Situations, struggles, and wins to bring up in session:

_____
_____
_____
_____
_____
_____
_____
_____
_____
_____
_____
_____

Homework and realizations to sit with before next session:

_____
_____
_____
_____
_____
_____
_____
_____
_____
_____
_____
_____

Date: _____

Situations, struggles, and wins to bring up in session:

_____
_____
_____
_____
_____
_____
_____
_____
_____
_____
_____
_____
_____

Homework and realizations to sit with before next session:

_____
_____
_____
_____
_____
_____
_____
_____
_____
_____
_____
_____
_____

Date: _____

Situations, struggles, and wins to bring up in session:

Homework and realizations to sit with before next session:

Date: _____

Situations, struggles, and wins to bring up in session:

_____
_____
_____
_____
_____
_____
_____
_____
_____
_____
_____

Homework and realizations to sit with before next session:

_____
_____
_____
_____
_____
_____
_____
_____
_____
_____
_____

Date: _____

Situations, struggles, and wins to bring up in session:

_____
_____
_____
_____
_____
_____
_____
_____
_____
_____
_____
_____

Homework and realizations to sit with before next session:

_____
_____
_____
_____
_____
_____
_____
_____
_____
_____
_____

Date: _____

Situations, struggles, and wins to bring up in session:

_____
_____
_____
_____
_____
_____
_____
_____
_____
_____
_____
_____
_____
_____

Homework and realizations to sit with before next session:

_____
_____
_____
_____
_____
_____
_____
_____
_____
_____
_____
_____
_____
_____

Date: _____

Situations, struggles, and wins to bring up in session:

Homework and realizations to sit with before next session:

Date: _____

Situations, struggles, and wins to bring up in session:

_____
_____
_____
_____
_____
_____
_____
_____
_____
_____
_____
_____

Homework and realizations to sit with before next session:

_____
_____
_____
_____
_____
_____
_____
_____
_____
_____

Date: _____

Situations, struggles, and wins to bring up in session:

_____
_____
_____
_____
_____
_____
_____
_____
_____
_____
_____
_____

Homework and realizations to sit with before next session:

_____
_____
_____
_____
_____
_____
_____
_____
_____
_____
_____
_____

Date: _____

Situations, struggles, and wins to bring up in session:

_____
_____
_____
_____
_____
_____
_____
_____
_____
_____
_____
_____

Homework and realizations to sit with before next session:

_____
_____
_____
_____
_____
_____
_____
_____
_____
_____
_____
_____

Date: _____

Situations, struggles, and wins to bring up in session:

_____
_____
_____
_____
_____
_____
_____
_____
_____
_____
_____
_____

Homework and realizations to sit with before next session:

_____
_____
_____
_____
_____
_____
_____
_____
_____
_____
_____

Date: _____

Situations, struggles, and wins to bring up in session:

_____
_____
_____
_____
_____
_____
_____
_____
_____
_____
_____

Homework and realizations to sit with before next session:

_____
_____
_____
_____
_____
_____
_____
_____
_____
_____
_____

Date: _____

Situations, struggles, and wins to bring up in session:

_____
_____
_____
_____
_____
_____
_____
_____
_____
_____

Homework and realizations to sit with before next session:

_____
_____
_____
_____
_____
_____
_____
_____
_____
_____

Date: _____

Situations, struggles, and wins to bring up in session:

Homework and realizations to sit with before next session:

Date: _____

Situations, struggles, and wins to bring up in session:

_____
_____
_____
_____
_____
_____
_____
_____
_____
_____
_____
_____
_____

Homework and realizations to sit with before next session:

_____
_____
_____
_____
_____
_____
_____
_____
_____
_____
_____
_____
_____

Date: _____

Situations, struggles, and wins to bring up in session:

Homework and realizations to sit with before next session:

Date: _____

Situations, struggles, and wins to bring up in session:

_____
_____
_____
_____
_____
_____
_____
_____
_____
_____
_____
_____
_____

Homework and realizations to sit with before next session:

_____
_____
_____
_____
_____
_____
_____
_____
_____
_____
_____
_____

Date: _____

Situations, struggles, and wins to bring up in session:

Homework and realizations to sit with before next session:

Date: _____

Situations, struggles, and wins to bring up in session:

_____
_____
_____
_____
_____
_____
_____
_____
_____
_____
_____
_____

Homework and realizations to sit with before next session:

_____
_____
_____
_____
_____
_____
_____
_____
_____
_____
_____
_____

Date: _____

Situations, struggles, and wins to bring up in session:

_____
_____
_____
_____
_____
_____
_____
_____
_____
_____
_____
_____
_____

Homework and realizations to sit with before next session:

_____
_____
_____
_____
_____
_____
_____
_____
_____
_____
_____
_____
_____

Date: _____

Situations, struggles, and wins to bring up in session:

_____
_____
_____
_____
_____
_____
_____
_____
_____
_____
_____
_____

Homework and realizations to sit with before next session:

_____
_____
_____
_____
_____
_____
_____
_____
_____
_____
_____
_____

Date: _____

Situations, struggles, and wins to bring up in session:

_____
_____
_____
_____
_____
_____
_____
_____
_____
_____

Homework and realizations to sit with before next session:

_____
_____
_____
_____
_____
_____
_____
_____
_____
_____

Date: _____

Situations, struggles, and wins to bring up in session:

_____
_____
_____
_____
_____
_____
_____
_____
_____
_____
_____
_____
_____

Homework and realizations to sit with before next session:

_____
_____
_____
_____
_____
_____
_____
_____
_____
_____
_____
_____
_____

Date: _____

Situations, struggles, and wins to bring up in session:

_____
_____
_____
_____
_____
_____
_____
_____
_____
_____
_____
_____

Homework and realizations to sit with before next session:

_____
_____
_____
_____
_____
_____
_____
_____
_____
_____
_____
_____

Date: _____

Situations, struggles, and wins to bring up in session:

_____
_____
_____
_____
_____
_____
_____
_____
_____
_____
_____
_____

Homework and realizations to sit with before next session:

_____
_____
_____
_____
_____
_____
_____
_____
_____
_____
_____
_____

Date: _____

Situations, struggles, and wins to bring up in session:

_____
_____
_____
_____
_____
_____
_____
_____
_____
_____
_____
_____

Homework and realizations to sit with before next session:

_____
_____
_____
_____
_____
_____
_____
_____
_____
_____
_____

Date: _____

Situations, struggles, and wins to bring up in session:

_____
_____
_____
_____
_____
_____
_____
_____
_____
_____
_____
_____

Homework and realizations to sit with before next session:

_____
_____
_____
_____
_____
_____
_____
_____
_____
_____
_____
_____

Date: _____

Situations, struggles, and wins to bring up in session:

_____
_____
_____
_____
_____
_____
_____
_____
_____
_____
_____

Homework and realizations to sit with before next session:

_____
_____
_____
_____
_____
_____
_____
_____
_____
_____
_____

Date: _____

Situations, struggles, and wins to bring up in session:

_____
_____
_____
_____
_____
_____
_____
_____
_____
_____
_____
_____
_____

Homework and realizations to sit with before next session:

_____
_____
_____
_____
_____
_____
_____
_____
_____
_____
_____
_____

Date: _____

Situations, struggles, and wins to bring up in session:

_____
_____
_____
_____
_____
_____
_____
_____
_____
_____
_____

Homework and realizations to sit with before next session:

_____
_____
_____
_____
_____
_____
_____
_____
_____
_____
_____
_____

Date: _____

Situations, struggles, and wins to bring up in session:

_____
_____
_____
_____
_____
_____
_____
_____
_____
_____
_____
_____
_____

Homework and realizations to sit with before next session:

_____
_____
_____
_____
_____
_____
_____
_____
_____
_____
_____

Date: _____

Situations, struggles, and wins to bring up in session:

_____
_____
_____
_____
_____
_____
_____
_____
_____
_____
_____
_____

Homework and realizations to sit with before next session:

_____
_____
_____
_____
_____
_____
_____
_____
_____
_____
_____
_____

Date: _____

Situations, struggles, and wins to bring up in session:

_____
_____
_____
_____
_____
_____
_____
_____
_____
_____
_____
_____

Homework and realizations to sit with before next session:

_____
_____
_____
_____
_____
_____
_____
_____
_____
_____
_____
_____

Date: _____

Situations, struggles, and wins to bring up in session:

_____
_____
_____
_____
_____
_____
_____
_____
_____
_____
_____
_____

Homework and realizations to sit with before next session:

_____
_____
_____
_____
_____
_____
_____
_____
_____
_____
_____
_____
_____

www.ingramcontent.com/pod-product-compliance
Lightning Source LLC
Chambersburg PA
CBHW050332010526
44119CB00004B/130